Lustre's

Little Blue Book

On Women and Retirement.

I0559032

Erica Baird & Karen E. Wagner

2nd edition

M·P·P
www.MissionPointPress.com

Mission Point Press

Published by Mission Point Press
MissionPointPress.com
PO Box 700028
Plymouth, MI 48170

ISBN: 9781968761110

Photography: Peter van Agtmael/Magnum Photos

Printed in the United States of America

Why Lustre.
Why This Little Book.

For many career women, retirement comes as a shock. It did for us. It wasn't that we didn't know it was coming. We did. And financially, we had planned for it. But we were not prepared for the discombobulation that came from being severed suddenly from our work and our careers.

We began to realize we are new, the first generation of women who forged careers and are now retiring in greater numbers than ever before. We are the role models for what's next. We also came to understand that, thanks to science and medicine, we have a 30-year runway. And yet, we are invisible.

So we started Lustre to remind members of this remarkable community how extraordinary we are, and to tell the world we are here—and we are not done. We want to inspire women like us to reject outdated notions of retirement and create a modern post-career paradigm. We are a new breed, and we will build a new path.

This small book puts some of our thoughts in a concise form. It reflects what we have learned from other Lustre women navigating the retirement journey and creating exciting new adventures. The wisdom of this cohort is palpable, and their energy is inspiring. This book will give you a taste of what is to come.

Erica and Karen
2025
www.lustre.net

Part I
The Shock.

You will not determine my story—I will.
-*Amy Schumer*

**Nothing in life is to be feared;
it is only to be understood.**

-Marie Curie

Before You Retire.

Don't worry if you don't have a plan.

Put something on the calendar for right after you retire. Someone to meet, some place to be.

Celebrate your successful career.

Don't panic.

You will figure it out.

When one door is shut,
another opens.

-*Miguel de Cervantes*

The Day You Retire.

This day will be over soon.

The only thing that ends is your job.

This is the beginning of the next third of your life.

You are the same vibrant, engaged and engaging person you were yesterday.

Champagne will help.

This World is not Conclusion.
A Species stands beyond-
Invisible, as Music-
But positive, as Sound-

-Emily Dickinson

Mourn.
It is part of the process.

You loved your career. You're sad it's over.

The sudden loss of structure and status is unnerving.

You don't see your people every day. You miss them.

There's no automatic *what's next.*

It's scary, but you're not alone. We all go through this.

Nothing is impossible,
the word itself says,
"I'm possible!"

-*Audrey Hepburn*

**The First Months.
What to Do.**

Sleep late. Lounge around.
Binge watch.

Find a retired friend to hang out with.

Go out. Dress up. Be seen.

Have fun. Do things you never had time to do before.

Say *yes* to (almost) everything.

Part II
Taking Control.

Accept the reality, embrace the challenge, and deal with it. Be in charge of your own life.

-Diane von Furstenberg

When there are no ceilings, the sky's the limit.

-Hillary Clinton

Take Control.

Your time is your own. You earned the right to control it.

Try new things. Be prepared to walk away.

Do not make momentous commitments until you're sure. Go slow.

The fact that you don't have a job does not mean you're everyone's gofer.
Just say *no*.

Relax. Breathe.

Hide not your talents,
They for use were made.
What's a sundial in the shade?

-Benjamin Franklin

What to Say When They Ask, "What Do You Do?"

Do not say, *I just retired* and then stop.

Do not say, *Nothing.*

Do say, *I am considering options.*
If you don't have any yet, fake it.

Do talk about your passions.

Do not retreat. Stay in the mix.

That the birds of worry and care fly above your head – this you cannot change. That they build nests in your hair – this you can prevent.

-*Chinese Proverb*

Be Visible.
Style Your Retirement.

Stand tall. Shoulders back.

Radiate confidence.

Dress differently but dress.

Find your voice. You have plenty to say.

Be bold. Courage is stylish.

In olden days, a glimpse of stocking
Was looked on as something shocking
But now, heaven knows,
Anything goes.

-Cole Porter

What to Wear Post-Suits.

Black leather. Motorcycle jacket?

Glittery flats or sneakers.

Dress jeans.

A colorful purse–cross body and just big enough for what you need now.

A white V-neck tee.

You're always believing ahead of your evidence. What was the evidence I could write a poem? I just believed it.

-Robert Frost

Identity. The Challenge.

Your job ended. You didn't.

Your work was a big part of you.
But not all of you.

Figure out what you want to do now.

Once you do, your new identity
will emerge.

It will take time.

Part III
Your New Age.

Beauty begins the moment you decide to be yourself.

-Coco Chanel

I just want to be wonderful.

-Marilyn Monroe

Seventy is the New Seventy.

Women in their 70s are future-facing.

A century ago, 50 was old. 70 was miraculous.

Today, 70 is simply elegant.

From 70, the future looks brilliant.

Take your age and run with it.

You can't help getting older, but you don't have to get old.

-George Burns

Your Runway Is Long.

If you retired in your 60s, you likely have 30 fabulous years ahead of you.

These three decades are a gift.

Use the gift to do amazing things— stimulating for you and inspiring for others.

Women over 60 have the drive, experience, wisdom and perspective to change the world. And we will.

If I have to, I can do
anything. I am strong,
I am invincible,
I am woman.

-*Helen Reddy*

Five Fun Facts about Older and Retired Women.

There are more retired women than ever before.

Boomer women control trillions of disposable income.

Women over 50 are the wealthiest cohort in the country.

Women over 65 are likely to live until at least 90 – with their wits intact.

Boomer women will change the face of retirement.

The older I get, the
greater power I seem to
have to help the world.
I am like a snowball,
the further I am rolled,
the more I gain.

-*Susan B. Anthony*

Own Your Age.

Be proud of your age. Tell everyone:
This is what my age looks like.

If people say you're too old for something,
just laugh.

Remember your superpower: experience.

Whatever your age, you are not old.

Remind people the only way to avoid
getting older is not worth it.

Fashion is instant language.

-Miuccia Prada

Dress Your Age.

Wear what you please.

Take risks if you are so inclined.

Wear elegant clothes to the outdoor market.

Wear elegant clothes to the bar when you meet your girlfriends and, if the occasion presents itself, flirt.

If you see your reflection in a shop window, nod to your confident self.

Part IV
Identity. Who Are You Now.

I can be changed by what happens to me.
But I refuse to be reduced by it.

-Maya Angelou

Leisure is a beautiful garment, but it will not do for constant wear.

-George Eliot

Finding Purpose.

Could you just play golf
and canasta–for decades?

If not, what do you want to
accomplish now?

Use your career and your passions
to guide you.

If you can't find just the right thing,
create it.

Trial and error is part of the journey.

The secret of change
is to focus all of your
energy, not on fighting
the old, but on building
the new.

-Socrates

Building a New Community.

Your job community is gone.
You need a new one for your new life.

Reach out to people you know.

Ask for introductions to people you
don't know.

Go places where you might meet
interesting people.

Try to meet in person when you can.
Remote is a last resort.

Around here, however, we don't look backwards for very long. We keep moving forward, opening up new doors and doing new things, because we're curious...and curiosity keeps leading us down new paths.

-*Walt Disney*

Where To Look For Your People.

Classes. Preferably in person. People like you will likely attend classes during the day.

Non-profits. Passionate about their mission? Do they have a need for your skills?

Group Travel. Demographics? All women? Some or all solo travelers? Age range? Ask.

Group workspaces. Find space to work outside your home and meet new people there.

Work. Want to be an entrepreneur? A flight attendant? Work in a bookstore? Do it.

A person who never
made a mistake never
tried anything new.

-Albert Einstein

Consider New Behaviors.

Strike up a conversation with a stranger. In line, on an airplane, in a museum.

Say *yes* to doing something new. Ballooning anyone?

Say *no* or *I quit*. Because you can.

Go to a bar or cafe by yourself. Sit next to someone you don't know. Start talking or look open to it.

Travel without a companion.

Dress to be noticed.

Stein: What is the answer?
Toklas: [Silence]
Stein: In that case, what is
the question?

-Gertrude Stein/Alice B. Toklas

Where do you want to live.

You can live anywhere. What's it going to be?

House? Apartment? Ship? Yurt?

The familiar or the exotic?

Urban? Suburban? Beach? Woods?

Hot? Cold? Just right?

Near your family? Or far?

Optimism is the faith that leads to achievement. Nothing can be done without hope and confidence.

-Helen Keller

Who You Are Now.

You are who you choose to be.

The person you have become is part of who you will be. Keep evolving.

Be someone who inspires, teaches, loves, creates, lives large.

Be remarkable. Maybe in a different way.

Keep creating yourself.

Part V
Retirement Surprises.

Happiness is the only thing that
multiplies when you share it.

-Albert Schweitzer

A woman is like a tea bag—you can't tell how strong she is until you put her in hot water.

-Eleanor Roosevelt

What Have We Learned Since We Founded Lustre?

Millions of women are retiring, and many feel like we do about what's next.

They miss their careers and want to remain part of the wider world.

But not everyone.

If you are one of those lucky women who were happy from the moment they retired—Congratulations!

If not, know you are in good company!

You can't use up creativity.
The more you use, the more
you have.

-Maya Angelou

After you retire, you could:

Write a play and get it produced on Broadway.

Found a dance company for people over 60—and travel the world.

Volunteer for a child advocacy organization.

Write murder mysteries—or a cookbook.

Put your grandmother's achievements on the map by writing about her textile career.

Aging is not "lost youth" but a new stage of opportunity and strength.

-*Betty Friedan*

You Will Figure It Out.

The best preparation for retirement is having a career you love.

You have so much experience. It will form the foundation of your new adventures.

The trick is to consider what you want to do, and then you will discover how to use your talents.

It is amazing how many people will want to help you.

You are entering an exhilarating time of your life.

When in doubt, breathe.

For all that has been, Thanks.
To all that shall be, Yes.

-*Dag Hammarskjöld*

Retirement Surprises.
Eventually.

Time is your new asset.

You've moved on. You actually don't want your old job back.

Your career is foundational in unexpected ways.

Retirement can be cool.

Retirement can empower the rebel in you.

After they retired, Erica and Karen founded Lustre to challenge stereotypes about retirement and older women and create a new framework for what modern retirement can look like. They are both lawyers who loved practicing law for over four decades. They were both firsts: Karen was the first female litigation partner in her global law firm, and Erica was the first female partner in the General Counsel's Office of a then-Big 8 accounting firm. Erica and Karen live on opposite ends of Manhattan.

You can reach Erica and Karen at info@lustre.net.

www.ingramcontent.com/pod-product-compliance
Lightning Source LLC
Chambersburg PA
CBHW051333120626
46547CB00016B/2527